S0-CJQ-335

My Best Moment

Four Personal Narratives

by Olivia Vega, Michael Martinoff,
Nadel Henville, and Kunal Rai

Table of Contents

Personal Narratives

What is a personal narrative?

A personal narrative is a nonfiction text that recreates an experience from the author's life. A personal narrative has a strong point of view, usually in the first person. It also communicates a distinct mood, or overall feeling. Most personal narratives are about something "big" in the author's life, such as a proud or sad moment, a trip or adventure, or an event that changed attitudes or actions.

What is the purpose of a personal narrative?

A personal narrative is a way to describe an experience so that others feel like they were there. Writers do this by using sensory details—what they saw, heard, touched, smelled, and tasted—and by including important events, characters, and dialogue. Writers explain what happened and also tell what they were thinking at the time and how they felt.

How do you read a personal narrative?

The title will likely give you a clue about the experience that the author will describe. As you read, pay close attention to the sequence of events. Ask yourself: *Did this event happen to the person, or did the person make it happen? How did this event affect the person's life? Is the author simply writing to entertain, or is there something that I can learn from his or her experience?*

A personal narrative focuses on one particular incident in the author's life.

A personal narrative may be a few paragraphs or several pages in length.

A personal narrative includes specific details about the time, place, and people involved.

Features of a Personal Narrative

A personal narrative includes the author's thoughts and feelings as well as the actual events.

A personal narrative includes dialogue.

Who writes personal narratives?

Everyone does! People record their experiences in diaries and journals, and share them in letters and e-mails. These informal writing opportunities provide valuable practice in selecting just the right details to make the experience come alive for others.

Meet the Authors

"My Brown-Eyed Babe"

Name: Olivia Vega

School: Wellington Christian Academy
Wellington, Kansas

About Me: I like to hang out with friends and I like to run. I want to be an artist or an author.

"The Hammock"

Name: Michael Martinoff

School: Grandhaven Elementary
McMinnville, Oregon

About Me: I like to play baseball and travel. My mom thinks I'm funny.

"Nazaih Arrives"

Name: Nadel Henville

School: Mayberry Elementary
East Hartford, Connecticut

About Me: I was born on the island of St. Lucia. I want to live in Paris when I grow up.

Tools Writers Use
A Strong Lead

A strong lead, or first sentence, grabs, or "hooks" the reader. A strong lead makes the reader want to keep reading. The lead describes something important about the topic without telling too much about the good parts to come. For personal narratives, writers usually use an indirect lead. An indirect lead may quote someone, ask a question, or describe a setting.

"The Catch"

Name: Kunal Rai

School: Old Union Elementary

Southlake, Texas

About Me: I would like to become an inventor and discover a way for all things to be powered by clean energy.

My Brown-Eyed Babe

D id Juliet know how cute she was? I patted her furry yellow head before I left to spend the night at my friend Lakin's house.

Juliet is an English setter. She's blond, with orange spots all over. She has the **floppiest** ears ever! I just wish she wasn't one of those dogs that looks kind of sad all the time. It was a time to be happy!

Juliet had her own home in the garage with her own pillow, blanket, and doggy house. It may not have looked comfortable to us humans, but it was a palace for her.

When I came home the next day, my little brother, Isaiah, ran to me screaming, "Juliet had puppies! Six of them!" My heart was racing as I ran, slipping and sliding, to our garage.

I stopped right in front of the puppies. I looked them over carefully, happily. One caught my eye. Lying alone in a corner with her newborn eyes tightly shut was a black puppy with the **tiniest** brown eyebrows. I bent over to pick her up. Once she was in my arms, I knew she was going to be my dog. I whispered in her ear, "You are my puppy. I'll never let you go. You will be my brown-eyed babe."

The days went by, then weeks and months, too. For all that time, my brown-eyed babe sat either on my lap or by my side. When she was three months old, I thought of a name for her. It was kind of silly, but I thought it fit her perfectly. I picked her up and put her close to my face. "Maya Moo Mercedes," I said. Sure enough, after I said her name she licked my nose.

Maya had one sister and four brothers: Jewels was the sister; Max, Marshmallow, Julian, and Milkshake were her brothers.

One day my mom put her arm on my shoulder. "We're going to have a garage sale . . . and we're going to give away the puppies."

"What? No, not Maya!" I shouted, feeling a piece of my heart break. "Can't we keep her?" I pleaded, hoping against hope.

"Isaiah already asked to keep Max," Mom replied.

I couldn't believe it! After all the times I slept with Maya on the kitchen floor. All the time I spent making up a silly song for her. Was it all for nothing? "That's not fair!" I said, trying to change Mom's mind.

"I can't tell Isaiah 'no,' after I already told him 'yes,'" Mom explained.

"We can keep both!" I said. "That way no one gets let down! Come on, Mom! Please?" I said, whimpering.

Mom sighed. She saw how much I really loved that brown-eyed babe. "Okay," she finally said with a smile.

We prepared for the garage sale. On that big day, we set out all the dogs except Max and Maya. I held my breath as the first customers came. Would they want Juliet's puppies? They looked at the puppies, picked one up and said, "I'll take this one." It broke my heart that Julian was now gone. After only a few hours, not one puppy was left. Juliet had the right to feel sad now, I thought.

I picked up Maya from my lap and whispered, "I will *never* let you go, my brown-eyed babe." I brushed her fur and kissed her head. I laid her on her pillow and slowly closed the door behind me.

* * * * *

It's been over a year since Maya was born. She has been close beside me ever since. A few weeks ago, Maya gave birth to three little puppies. Her puppies are the most beautiful, **most precious** things I have ever seen. I fell in love with them, too. But no matter how many puppies she has, or how old she will grow, Maya will always be my brown-eyed babe.

Max on floor; Maya lying on Juliet

The Hammock

Do you have a special place where you can get away from everything and just relax? I do. It's the hammock in my family's backyard. My favorite time of year to be in the hammock is autumn. When I lie in the hammock then, I see the trees swaying, the leaves falling, and the **bluest** of skies. I love it when the red, yellow, and orange leaves float silently onto my face.

Sometimes I bring out my mp3 player and listen to music while I watch the leaves. When I don't bring my music, I just listen to the creak of the hammock as it sways back and forth, back and forth, while I watch the leaves. Ahh . . .

Occasionally, I bring out a book to read. In some books, there is a forest setting. Being in the hammock among the trees makes me feel like I'm in the forest in the book. If I'm reading an action scene in a story, I imagine that the good guys are jumping around and telling me, "The bad guys are weak. You can take them!"

I love the smell of the trees, too. I never realized before I lay there in the hammock that trees could smell so good. I like to close my eyes and sniff the air for the scent of pine trees. I breathe in deeply.

Once in a while, my dog Fritz, a beagle-labrador mix, hops up onto the hammock with me. The hammock will wobble for a couple of seconds and I have to steady it. My dog licks me. I pet him with the softest, **gentlest** strokes.

Your **most special** place doesn't have to be a hammock, but I do hope you find a place where you can drift away to another world.

Analyze the Narratives
- What experiences do these personal narratives describe?
- Where did they happen? How did each setting affect what happened?
- Which people were involved? How did these people affect what happened?
- How do the writers feel about their experiences now?

Analyze the Tools Writers Use: A Strong Lead
- What type of lead did Olivia use? Michael?
- Did the leads "hook" you as a reader? Why? How?
- What did you think the narratives were going to be about from the lead?

Focus on Words: Superlatives
Superlatives are special adjectives that are used to compare three or more things. Some superlatives end in **-est**, while others are preceded by the word **most**. Analyze the following superlatives from "My Brown-Eyed Babe" and "The Hammock."

Adjective	Superlative Form of the Adjective	Page
floppy	floppiest	6
tiny	tiniest	7
precious	most precious	9
blue	bluest	10
gentle	gentlest	12
special	most special	12

Nazaih Arrives

T he **greatest** day of my life was December 18, 2008. It was a cold, gray, drizzly day outside. But inside I was a burst of sunshine. That was the day that my nephew Nazaih was born! Although this was not my first time as an aunt, it was the first time I went to the hospital to see the newborn baby.

We were so eager to see my sister Natalia and my nephew. At first, we couldn't find the right room. That was our **most anxious** moment. Then we found the room. Baby presents were all over the floor. My sister was in bed. Nazaih was next to her. He looked like the tiniest baby ever, but he weighed eight pounds and eleven ounces. That's pretty big for a newborn.

I felt a little left out because everyone else in the room held him. It didn't matter that much to me though. I couldn't take my eyes off him. Nazaih had hazel eyes, soft, smooth skin and lots of hair. My family called him "Little Man" because he had the **hairiest** arms and legs. When he yawned, which was like every minute, my heart melted. He was so adorable that I could not stop staring.

Natalia was in pain, so we needed to let her be. It wasn't until later in the day that I got to see my little Nazaih again. As I looked at him, I started to imagine what he would be like as a toddler. I saw him playing with a basketball set, laughing. I thought about all the games I would play with him, like hide and seek.

When I went home, I felt a new kind of happiness. It was like a dark hole in me was now filled up with Nazaih.

The Catch

A chilly wind blew through Bicentennial Park on that Saturday night in October 2007. My baseball team, the Raptors, was playing the Mountain Cats in the league semifinals. The Mountain Cats were the **toughest** team in the league. It was do-or-die for us.

Despite the cool weather, both teams came out swinging. By the sixth inning the score was 13–12. We were on top! Now it was the Mountain Cats' last licks. We took the field determined not to let the other team scare us or shake our spirit. We got one out, then another. Then the Cats loaded the bases! What's worse, their **fiercest** hitter, Jack, was up. He walked onto the field swinging his bat. The crowd cheered him on as he walked toward the plate. Our stony determination began to show some cracks.

The author focuses on one specific event. The actual incident that inspired this personal narrative, a baseball game, was only a couple of hours in the author's life.

Jack took his place at the plate and adjusted his stance. The lights flickered and the crowd went quiet. Tyler, our pitcher, wound up and threw a fastball right down the middle. "Strike one," yelled the umpire.

In center field, I took more than a few steps back. I could tell that Jack was going for a homer.

Tyler threw a ball down the middle again. *Crack!* The baseball zoomed past Tyler and kept on going. The lights flickered again and the crowd roared. The ball was coming my way! I was the most nervous person on the field. I ran forward, then backward. I wasn't sure where the ball would land. The crowd grew silent once more.

Here the author shares his thoughts and feelings while he was on the field, as well as the actual events that occurred.

I jumped into the air and felt something hit my glove. Then I hit the ground with a thud. *Thump!* I skidded. I rolled. My jersey was covered with dirt and grass. I was afraid to look in my glove. As I saw my other team members jump in excitement and run toward me, I looked into the glove and saw the ball!

Using sound words helps readers feel as if they're right there with the author.

"Out!" yelled the umpire. I leapt into the air and did a 1440 spin (that's four 360 degree spins). My teammates jumped for joy and came to give me a group hug. The umpire indicated that the game was over. The Raptors had won. Both teams came out of the dugouts to shake hands with each other.

The author brings in other people that were at the event, and uses dialogue and detailed descriptions to help place the readers in the middle of the action.

As we do after every game, our team gathered around our coach to review the game. We bubbled over with excitement to have reached the finals. It had been a long, hard road for the team. The coach handed me the game ball as I was voted MVP for the game. I still wasn't sure if it had all been a dream.

A personal narrative is about an experience that has a deep, personal meaning for the author. In the end, the author shares how he felt after the experience and his hopes for the future.

Afterward, everyone started to leave the stadium. Making the catch for my team was one of the **most phenomenal** experiences of my life. As I was going home, I wondered if I would be able to catch the ball like that again. There wasn't much else I could do but keep practicing and hope for another chance.

Kunal keeps the ball he caught as a memory of his best moment.

Reread the Personal Narratives

Analyze the Narratives
- What experiences do these personal narratives describe?
- Where did they happen? How did each setting affect what happened?
- Which people were involved? How did these people affect what happened?
- How do the writers feel about their experiences now?

Analyze the Tools Writers Use: A Strong Lead
- What type of lead did Nadel use? Kunal?
- Did the leads "hook" you as a reader? Why? How?
- What did you think the narrative was going to be about from the lead?

Focus on Words: Superlatives
Superlatives are special adjectives that are used to compare three or more things. Some superlatives end in **-est**, while others are preceded by the word **most**. Analyze the following superlatives from "Nazaih Arrives" and "The Catch."

Adjective	Superlative Form of the Adjective	Page
great	greatest	14
anxious	most anxious	14
hairy	hairiest	15
tough	toughest	16
fierce	fiercest	17
phenomenal	most phenomenal	20

How does an author write a

Personal Narrative?

Reread "The Catch" and think about what Kunal Rai did to write this narrative. How did he keep a narrow focus? How did he make you feel like you were there?

(1.) Decide on an Experience

Remember: A personal narrative is an actual retelling of something you have experienced. Therefore, you will use words such as **I**, **me**, and **my** as you write. In "The Catch," the author wanted to tell about an amazing play he made for his baseball team.

(2.) Decide Who Else Needs to Be in Your Narrative

Often, other people—or even animals—were a part of your experience. Ask yourself:
• Who was there with me?
• Which people are important to my story?
• How will I describe these people?
• Which people should I leave out?
• Can I tell my story without embarrassing another person?
  If not, what other experience could I write about?

Person	Jack	Tyler	Umpire	Teammates and Coach
Importance to Story	fiercest hitter on the opposing team	pitcher on the author's team	called the batter out and let the players know the game was over	congratulated the author; gave him the MVP award

3. Recall Events and Setting

Jot down notes about what happened and where it happened. Ask yourself:
- Where did my experience take place? How will I describe it?
- What was the situation or problem I experienced? Was the experience happy, scary, sad, or surprising?
- What events happened?
- How did my experience turn out?
- What questions might my readers have about my experience that I could answer in my narrative?

Setting	Events	How My Experience Turned Out
Baseball field at Bicentennial Park **Situation or Problem** My team wanted to beat the Mountain Cats in the league semifinals.	1. The Cats' fiercest hitter was up when they were down by one run and had the bases loaded. 2. The hitter hit the ball straight out to center field where I stood. 3. I jumped into the air to catch the ball.	I caught it! We won the game, I got the MVP award, and our team got to go to the finals.

Glossary

bluest (BLOO-est) having the most color blue (page 10)

fiercest (FEER-sist) most terrifying (page 17)

floppiest (FLAH-pee-est) softest; loosest (page 6)

gentlest (JEN-tuh-lest) most delicate (page 12)

greatest (GRAY-test) best (page 14)

hairiest (HAIR-ee-est) having the most hair (page 15)

most anxious (MOST ANK-shus) most worrisome (page 14)

most phenomenal (MOST fih-NAH-muh-nul) most amazing (page 20)

most precious (MOST PREH-shus) most cherished (page 9)

most special (MOST SPEH-shul) most valued (page 12)

tiniest (TY-nee-est) smallest (page 7)

toughest (TUH-fest) most challenging (page 16)

Make Connections Across Texts

Complete a graphic organizer like the one below.

Narrative	My Brown-Eyed Babe	The Hammock	Nazaih Arrives	The Catch
Situation				
People Involved				
Summary				

Analyzing the Narratives

Use your graphic organizer to help you answer these questions.

• How does each title prepare you for reading the personal narrative?

• What connections can you make to these personal narratives?

• How did you feel as you read each personal narrative?

• How are the personal narratives alike?

• How are the personal narratives different?

• What could readers learn from these personal narratives?

Four Personal Narratives

A favorite puppy... Peaceful times in a hammock... The birth of a nephew... A game-saving catch. Read about these kids' memorable moments. Then learn how to write one of your own.

Olivia Vega
lives in Kansas.

Michael Martinoff
lives in Oregon.

Nadel Henville
lives in Connecticut.

Kunal Rai
lives in Texas.

Enjoy all of these Nonfiction Readers' & Writers' Genre Workshop titles.

Biography

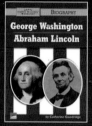

Informational Texts

Journals

Personal Narratives

Persuasive Letters

Procedural Texts

Reviews: Books

BENCHMARK EDUCATION COMPANY

ISBN 978-1-60859-627-0

9 781608 596270